Yarn Bombers

Story by Cameron Macintosh

Illustrations by Jane Pica

Yarn Bombers

Text: Cameron Macintosh
Publishers: Tania Mazzeo and Eliza Webb
Series consultant: Amanda Sutera
    Hands on Heads Consulting
Editor: Laken Ballinger
Project editor: Annabel Smith
Designer: Jess Kelly
Project designer: Danielle Maccarone
Illustrations: Jane Pica
Production controller: Renee Tome

NovaStar

Text © 2024 Cengage Learning Australia Pty Limited
Illustrations © 2024 Cengage Learning Australia Pty Limited

ISBN 978 0 17 033420 4

Cengage Learning Australia
Level 5, 80 Dorcas Street
Southbank VIC 3006 Australia
Phone: 1300 790 853
Email: aust.nelsonprimary@cengage.com

For learning solutions, visit **cengage.com.au**

Printed in China by 1010 Printing International Ltd
1 2 3 4 5 6 7 28 27 26 25 24

Nelson acknowledges the Traditional Owners and Custodians of the lands of all First Nations Peoples. We pay respect to Elders past and present, and extend that respect to all First Nations Peoples today.

Contents

Chapter 1

Community Week

It was Community Week at Kade's school. Kade and his classmates were learning about some of the organisations in their local area and all the work that they did. Every day, a different person came to speak to the class. Kade always had lots of questions for the speakers.

On Friday, Kade's teacher, Mr Roselli, introduced Sarah, the final speaker for the week. She was one of the managers of Homelands, a shelter that provided all sorts of help to people experiencing homelessness.

"Thanks for having me," said Sarah. "I'm looking forward to telling you about everything we do at Homelands."

"But first," said Sarah, "let me tell you what it means to be homeless. A person who is homeless doesn't have a safe or regular place to live. Some homeless people live in their cars. Many live on the streets."

The class listened quietly while Sarah told them that people can become homeless for all sorts of reasons. She explained that Homelands gave many people food and a safe place to sleep.

"How did you start working at Homelands?" asked Kade.

Sarah told the class that when she was younger, she had been homeless herself. That experience made her want to help other people going through difficult times.

"How can people help Homelands?" asked Tyler.

"Well," replied Sarah, "our biggest problem is that our blankets are old and raggedy, and winter is just around the corner."

Kade saw Mr Roselli's eyebrows rise. Mr Roselli picked up his tablet and made a note on it.

Chapter 2

A New Class Project

Later that morning, after Sarah had left, Mr Roselli said to his students, "The shelter needs new blankets, and I have an idea for how we can help to provide them."

"Would you like us all to donate some blankets?" asked Kade.

"Even better," replied Mr Roselli with a smile. "We're going to *make* the blankets!"

"But how?" asked Alex.

"By knitting them!" said Mr Roselli.

"But I don't know how to knit!" said Tyler.

"Don't worry, I'll show you!" replied Mr Roselli.

Mr Roselli explained that to knit, they needed to use two thick, long needles to join loops of yarn together. He assured the class that they would pick up the basic skills very quickly.

"But it'll take months for each of us to make our own blankets!" said Tyler.

Mr Roselli told the students that they'd only knit one square each. He would then join the squares together with yarn to make the blankets.

Kade leaned over towards Alex and Tyler. "I thought it was only old people who knit," he said quietly.

"I heard that!" said Mr Roselli. "Actually, people of all ages enjoy knitting, including students in Year Four!"

"My two brothers and I learned to do it when we were your age. We filled the house with scarves and blankets and colourful cushion covers."

"So," continued Mr Roselli, "we'll get started next Monday."

Everyone in the class seemed excited, except for the three boys at the front.

Tyler groaned as he, Kade and Alex walked outside at lunchtime. "I want to help the people at the shelter," he said, "but why can't we just raise money to *buy* some blankets? Then we could spend our time doing more interesting things than knitting."

"Yeah," said Alex. "I'd rather be practising my jumps at the skatepark."

"And I'd rather be at my desk, drawing cartoons!" said Kade.

Chapter 3

Learning to Knit

The following Monday morning, Mr Roselli handed out knitting needles and did a demonstration for the class. Some of the students already knew how to knit, but Kade and the others needed help to start their squares. After that, they were able to keep going on their own.

Every day for the rest of the week, the class spent half an hour working on their knitting project. Kade, Alex and Tyler were soon knitting as well as anyone, and they were enjoying it more than they wanted to admit!

By the end of the week, everyone's squares were finished. Mr Roselli then stitched them together to make two colourful, warm blankets. Everyone was so proud of the blankets. Mr Roselli invited Sarah back to the class to present them to her.

"Thanks, Year Fours!" said Sarah. "You're all very clever. Everyone at Homelands will love these."

But as Sarah was leaving, Kade overheard her speaking to Mr Roselli. "We may have to cut back on the meals we serve at the shelter," she said. "We don't have enough money to buy the food we need."

Oh, *no*, thought Kade. *We need to do something to help. But what?*

Chapter 4

A Day in the City

The next weekend, Kade, his mum and his sister, Tara, took the one-hour train ride into the city. Kade had been asking Mum to take him to see an exhibition of drawings by his favourite cartoonist.

As they rode on the train, Kade told Mum and Tara about the problems Sarah was having at the shelter.

"You all did such a great job with the blankets," said Mum. "I'm sure you'll think of something else that can help."

Walking back towards the train station that afternoon, Kade noticed some unusual colours on a tree they passed. He stopped to take a closer look, and he realised that the tree's trunk and two of its branches were covercd in knitted patches.

"Look at this!" he said to Tara. "I've never seen anything like it!"

"It's called yarn bombing," replied Tara. "My friend Ahmed does it. It's a form of street art. Artists make patches from yarn and wrap them around things like trees and poles to make them look more interesting."

Kade couldn't stop looking at the yarn-covered tree.

What a cool idea, he thought. *Maybe Mr Roselli is right – knitting isn't just for old people.*

As Kade sat on the train back home, his mind kept leaping back to the multicoloured tree he'd just seen. It soon gave him an idea for something the class could do to raise money for the shelter.

Chapter 5

Pay for a Patch

On Monday, Kade told everyone about the art of yarn bombing. He showed them photos of some other yarn-bombed objects he'd found online. He'd even come across photos of bikes that had been yarn bombed!

"This all gave me an idea," Kade said to the class. "The shelter still needs help, so why don't we use our knitting skills to 'yarn bomb' the old tree near the school gate? We could ask everyone in the school community to donate money for every patch we add to the tree. Then, we can give the money to Sarah at Homelands."

"That sounds like the perfect project for us," said Mr Roselli.

"Let's get knitting!" added Tyler.

That day after school, Kade went to the shelter with his mum and Mr Roselli. Kade told Sarah about his fundraising idea.

"It's called 'Pay for a Patch'," he said. "For a few dollars per patch, we'll yarn bomb the old tree near our school gate. It'll look amazing, and we'll raise lots of money to help you keep the shelter going."

"What a fantastic idea!" said Sarah.

Kade asked Mr Roselli if he could write an ad for the yarn-bombing project to go in the next school newsletter. Soon, the ad was emailed out to the entire school community.

Kade's mum also set up a page on her social media account, inviting people in their local area to pay for a patch.

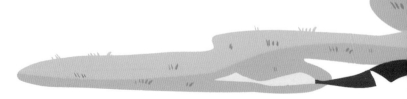

Over the next few weeks, Kade and his classmates spent much of their spare time knitting more squares. They soon had enough patches to cover the tree.
As people paid for the patches, Mr Roselli carefully added them to the tree trunk.

The students' hard work raised enough money to help Sarah buy six large boxes of canned and fresh food for the people at Homelands.

"Thanks again, Kade," said Sarah, admiring the colourful tree trunk. "It's people like you and your classmates who make this such a *tight-knit* community!"